SCARCITY

OF

SEAMEN.

SCARCITY OF SEAMEN.

SECOND EDITION.

In prosecuting the work of this mission, the attention of your Missionary has been drawn to the fact, of the increasing scarcity of Seamen. The subject is one of great importance when viewed in its relations to Commerce. It has also an intimate connection with the welfare of seamen, and underlies all plans for their improvement. On this latter account I have deemed it of sufficient importance to demand prominence in my Annual Report.

It has occurred to me, that possibly *something* might be done through the agency of this mission, towards diminishing this evil, and however small the contribution, if it should but increase the number of seamen, and promote their moral elevation as a class, it would well repay all the effort made. Under this impression, I propose to present first of all, facts, showing the extent of the evil; and then offer such suggestions in respect to the remedy, as have presented themselves to my mind while examining the subject, availing myself of many valuable hints from ship-owners and ship-masters in this and other ports of the United States; and using my own experience as a practical seaman and seamen's missionary, in so far as it may throw light on the subject. These I shall follow up, with a plan for increasing the number and efficiency of our *native marine*, which I shall commence forthwith to carry out in connection with my other labors.

CAUSES OF THE SCARCITY OF SEAMEN.

Several causes have contributed to produce the present scarcity of seamen; prominent among which is, the custom, widely prevailing, of sailing our merchant ships with able seamen, to the exclusion of *apprentices* or "green hands." This could be done without difficulty, so long as foreign sailors were abundant, and the offer of higher wages furnished inducement to abandon their own, and sail under the American flag. *Of late years foreign sailors have constituted three-fourths of our entire marine.* But the recent discoveries of gold, and the increasing commerce of the nations of Europe in a time of general peace, has created a demand for seamen in all parts of the world, and caused a rise in their wages, the effect of which has been, to cut off our supply of foreign sailors. At the last accounts, seamen's wages in England, were fully up to the ruling price in this country. This new state of things has been taken advantage of, and several popular outbreaks or *strikes* among seamen, for higher wages, have occurred in the ports of Great Britain. So great is the scarcity of seamen in the British Navy, that recently a new screw ship, commanded by Captain Keppel — a popular officer — *was detained fourteen weeks in obtaining one hundred and thirty men.* In a recent report of a Committee of Naval Officers, it was stated that not more than *twenty-one thousand* available seamen are to be found in the United Kingdom at any one time; and the British government, from the force of circumstances, are now resorting to new and hitherto untried measures, to induce seamen to enter the naval service. The case is no better with us. Speaking on this subject, a New York paper uses the following language: "There is no means of relieving the squadron on the Coast of Africa by another ship, because seamen cannot be got; the clipper ships strip Uncle Sam of his men." It is well known that the Japan Expedition was detained for want of men, and that great difficulty exists in obtaining a supply for the Home Squadron. A ship-master writing from New York, under date of December 13th, remarks: "The Navy are about to make a desperate effort to get men by raising the pay;" and adds, "It will be a great burden on the merchant service, to have the nation outbid the merchant, paying out the public money in such sums as to make competition ruinous."

Another cause of the scarcity of seamen will be found in the *desertions* from our own, and the ships of other countries in the gold regions. A New York paper, in treating of this subject, says, "*It is calculated that the Pacific Ocean service, absorbs four thousand seamen every year*, that is to say, that number go out from the Atlantic, and do not return; some going to California or Australia, others lingering in the Islands, or perishing; there is no adequate supply for such an absorption, and hence the scarcity of seamen." To this statement might be added the fact, that of those who return to the Atlantic Ports, many of them enter our hospitals to die; while some are so broken in constitution, or debased in moral character, as ever afterwards to prove either useless, or a moral pest on board every vessel in which they sail.

It may be well to remark here, that the Whale Fisheries furnish much fewer seamen to our merchant marine than is generally supposed; the employment is not attractive, either on the score of compensation for labor, or as a means for gratifying the desire of travel. To many of our young men it has proved a deep sea lottery, with more blanks than prizes. As far as seeing the world is concerned, it is a world of waters, of which adventurous spirits soon tire; large numbers of young men who enter this service are satisfied with a single voyage, and leave the ocean, never to return. Even in the merchant service, this is oft times the case, not a few of the better sort of young men, become disgusted with forecastle life on account of its depraved character, and seize the first favorable moment to free themselves from its contamination.

Another cause of the scarcity of seamen, is, *the multiplication of clipper ships, requiring large crews.* From tables connected with the report of the Secretary of the Treasury, for 1852, it appears—that the average annual increase in size or tonnage, of vessels built in the States of Maine, New Hampshire, Massachusetts and New York, for the previous sixteen years, was at the rate of 28½ per cent.; while from 1849 to 1852, three years, (the last year inclusive,) it was 66 per centum per annum.

In connection with the causes named, is, *the constant diminution by death.* An estimate made at Lloyd's, London, fixes the life of seamen at an average of 11½ years from their commencing to go to sea, or an annual decrease by death of 8¾ per cent. The tonnage of the United States for the year 1852, foreign and coastwise—gross estimate—was 4,000,000 tons; that of Great Britain, for the year 1853, was 4,424,000 tons, and employed 243,512 men and boys, or 5½ persons for every 100 tons of shipping. Allowing to our own vessels 3½ persons to the 100 tons, or less than two-thirds the complement of British crews, and our marine will number 140,000, exclusive of the naval service; subtract from this number 8¾ per cent. annual decrease by death, and it amounts to 12,250; add to this one half of the number supposed to be absorbed in the Pacific, say 2000, *and there is a loss to us of* 14,250 *seamen annually.*

The Secretary of State of the United States, reports the increase of seamen by Registry, for the year 1852, at 9798, which, compared with the annual decrease as estimated above, *leaves the annual deficiency of about* 4500 *seamen.* The Registry is without doubt a fair exhibit of the annual increase of our native marine, although the impression prevails to some extent, that in the coasting trade, and the cod and mackerel fisheries, a large number of American seamen are employed, who are not Registered, and who would, therefore, be overlooked in a general estimate. So far from this being the case, three-fourths of those engaged in the coasting trade, and one half of all our fishermen, are computed to be foreigners; of the balance, it may be safely affirmed, that a large majority of them are registered seamen, who divide their time between fishing, coasting and foreign voyages.

Having considered the subject of the scarcity of seamen, and noted some of the causes, it remains to be seen whether there is not some effectual remedy for this great evil— What then is

THE REMEDY.

It may be safely assumed, that we have abundant means for meeting this exigency, if we will employ them; what the means are, and how they shall be used, are important questions to be considered. A New York paper alluding to this subject, says, "The supply of seamen has been short for a long time past, and it is believed by those familiar with the subject must remain so, until our ships consent to take a certain proportion of boys, (as apprentices,) to make up their crews; a great many boys offer themselves, but are generally rejected." One of our city papers uses the following language on the same subject:—"The race of American seamen is fast becoming extinct, and unless some remedy is immediately applied, the flag of our country will soon be upheld by foreigners." In this last quotation, both the evil and the remedy are stated with force, and clearness. We want then, a new race of American seamen, in whom we can repose confidence; the pecuniary interests involved in our vast commercial relations, demand such, no less than the comfort and safety of the increasing multitudes of travellers by sea; especially do we need such a race of seamen as the fitting representatives of a great, commercial, Christian nation. In justice to foreign sailors, it may be said with truth, that there are among them some of the best specimens of seamen that sail under the American flag; as officers, too, they hold a deservedly high rank. While this is true, there are others of the most depraved character. To attempt to discriminate between the different nations represented on board our vessels, would be invidious and unnecessary; every ship-master knows where the difference lies. There is some doubt whether, morally considered, every American sailor is just what he should be, although this is not the place to discuss that question; *but whether foreign sailors are good or bad, better or worse than our own seamen, they are fast failing us, and it is no longer a question of choice between the two, but whether we will have American sailors, or lay our vessels up at the wharves!* If we then conclude to raise up a native marine, how is it to be done, and what shall be its character? Two modes for meeting the exigency present themselves, one of which, we must choose. The first to be considered, is—

A MARINE APPRENTICESHIP SYSTEM.

Much has been said and written on this subject of late, but no practical plan has yet appeared. Indeed, it may well be doubted, whether a system of marine apprenticeship can be devised, that will meet the wants of our commercial and naval service; the attempt made in the navy, commencing about the year 1840—to educate and discipline boys for the navy—signally failed. The principal difficulty in the way of marine apprenticeship, in this country, is, that it is not in unison with the genius and spirit of our Institutions and people. The system of Great Britain, with which we are most familiar, is objectionable, on the ground of its compulsory features; it encroaches on personal liberty. The condition and wants of Great Britain, however, are different from those of this country; there, a coercive system may be best, the PRESS GANG included; there, where "the overseers of the poor for any parish, are authorized to bind any boy who may have attained the age of 12 years, to the sea service, provided such boy consents to be bound," (a happy deliverance for the pauper boy,) it may work well. But we have seen enough of this class of pauper sailors, to cure us of any desire to witness the adoption of the system among us. Surely, intelligent, free America, requires better materials for her merchant and naval marine, than are furnished by either the prisons or poor houses of the land; besides, a system of coerced labor cannot compete with that which is free. The seven years legal apprenticeship, which prevailed in New England fifty years ago, has been abandoned for the voluntary system, of labor and compensation, graduated upon a scale of increasing ability. With such advantages of employment *on the land*, with freedom of will and of action, it is not to be expected that a legal apprenticeship AT SEA, abridging personal liberty, will have commanding attractions for the high-spirited youth of our country. One other difficulty remains to be noticed: The apprenticeship act of Great Britain,* "makes it lawful for the master of an apprentice, or in case of the master's death, his executor or administrator, with the consent of the apprentice, if above seventeen years of age, to assign or transfer the indenture to any other master or owner. Some trouble would probably be met with, in carrying out such a provision here — where property is widely distributed, and joint ownership in vessels, almost universal. And yet, no system will be complete, or of any practical benefit without it. Who, then, it may be asked, on the apprenticeship plan, is to be master to the apprentice; shall it be one of the many owners, or the ship, or the captain? And when the vessel changes owners and captain, what then is the position of the apprentice, to whom does he owe service? It will not be easy to reconcile these conflicting interests, and less so to obtain the consent of an intelligent youth, voluntarily to put himself into such a position. If then, an apprenticeship system is not the remedy for the evil, probably it may be met by

THE VOLUNTARY SYSTEM.

This contemplates a native marine, to be created out of volunteers or green-hands, who commence a sea life young, in the merchant service, which is the proper place to learn seaman's duties. The plan briefly stated, is as follows:— To open an Intelligence Office in each of our large seaports, where, on application, youth of good character may learn of an employ, and ship-owners and ship-masters may find youth of the right stamp for their vessels, as set forth particularly in a circular published in connection with this Report. The plan proposes that every vessel take a proportion of green hands, at the discretion of owners and officers, to be selected by a competent person devoted to the interests of the owners, to be treated as *wards* of the ship, and protected in their rights, persons and property, and dealt with in a way to make them high minded, honorable men, and good sailors, and with the understanding, if it prove mutually advantageous, that they are to serve a term of from three to five years, or until they are twenty-one years of age, with the prospect of promotion and permanent employ thereafter. That during the whole period of service they are to be considered as belonging to the ship, and identified with their owners and employers, and under pay; receiving

* Entitled, "The Merchant Seamen's Act, 8th Victoria," now repealed.

such rate of wages as may be agreed upon, with an allowance for board on shore when it shall be for the interest or convenience of the employer, with such privilege of visiting home in the interval between voyages, as may be reasonable and proper. When at length the term of voluntary apprenticeship, (for such it is,) shall expire, that a Certificate be furnished them by their employers, of good character, ability, and faithfulness, to be registered in the Custom House of the District sailed from, and which in addition to its value as a means for helping them forward in the merchant service, shall entitle them ever after, to the highest wages as *able seamen* in the navy of the United States, and to the consideration of the Naval Board as candidates for promotion in the naval service. Let these terms of *voluntary apprenticeship* become general, and there is strong ground for believing that the character of seamen will soon be redeemed from the reproaches now heaped upon them; for it is in the use of such means, and through their influence, that men, living in the bosom of society, become honest, industrious, ambitious, thrifty and moral. It is too much to expect of sailors, that they will be as good as other men, when the means for making them so are left unemployed.

HOW THE VOLUNTARY SYSTEM WILL WORK.

It cannot be expected that the above plan will, in every instance, produce the exact result desired; this would be more than is realized in the working of the system on shore. How is it in the contract between the merchant and the clerk, the mechanic and his apprentice? Sometimes the youth proves too ambitious for his own good, and desires change, or mistakes his calling, and wisely abandons it. Sometimes employers are parsimonious—exacting—dishonorable, and the youth of becoming spirit, prefers defeat in an attempt to do better, rather than remain, to be imposed upon. At other times, employers are honorable men and gentlemen, while those who represent them in their business are neither the one nor the other, and a rupture is the consequence. And not unfrequently, superior attainments on the part of a youth, engaged in a particular employ, may lead a third party to desire his services with increased pay, and unjust and dishonest interference.

These are the drawbacks to the system on shore. And yet this class of contracts are made every day, and the principle is held to be fundamental in every department of business. Our best merchants, mechanics, and traders, are produced in this way, and no one thinks of abandoning the system for its exceptive working. There is reason for believing, that were the classes just named, in securing the ends of their several callings, to abandon the present mode, and resort to the employment of unknown, untried and irresponsible agents, as is the custom in our merchant marine, that it could not fail to endanger their success to an alarming extent. The only reason why less apparent injury is experienced in navigation, in pursuing such a course, is, that the losses accruing are provided for, in increased rates of insurance and higher freights. It is submitted whether the voluntary system — shown to be beneficial on shore — if closely adhered to, would not work even better in the sea service; seeing that in no other employment, at the present day, is there equal promise of promotion and success in life.

As regards the term of service — three or five years — less or more, it cannot but affect the working of the system favorably. The certificate of an able seaman, which it is supposed will not be given irrespective of desert, may be earned in some cases in a short period of time; in others, it will require more. A standard of able seamanship is necessary, and the period of majority is the best that can be selected. But should a youth, commencing a sea life early, be ambitious to attain to an officer's berth, before reaching *legal* manhood — no unusual circumstance in our merchant service — the system will not interfere with the accomplishing of his object. He will simply prove himself to be of the class of honorable exceptions, not provided for by the system, which is especially designed for the benefit of the great body of seamen, who may be less ambitious, or less successful.

BUT ONE SERIOUS DIFFICULTY.

The only serious difficulty to be encountered in carrying out the Voluntary System, is, the false views and reasonings prevalent, on the subject of the sailor's character and employments. The idea seems to be — that sailors are a species of *amphibi*, with whom you cannot deal on common principles, and that their employments only make them worse and worse. If this were true, then, indeed, there would be no hope; but it is not. The real ground of effort and of hope in the case, is the fact, that the sailor is capable of appreciating the highest obligations of a contract.

The class of youth from which it is proposed to raise up an efficient marine, are imbued with a passion for the sea, and are generally above the average of mind, education and social position. The passion for the sea alluded to, is but the working out of a great law of our being. Our youth desire to go to sea, from an instinctive impression of its adaptedness to promote their happiness, and meet the highest wants of their nature, and in this they are not mistaken. The ocean *is* adapted to high intellectual, social and moral development. First, the employments of the sea demand skill, ingenuity and intellectual ability, in a far greater degree than the purely mechanical employments on shore. Next, a well regulated ship affords ample opportunity for intellectual and social culture. As regards the imagery of the sea, it is in the highest degree suggestive and ennobling. It is to the ocean, the painter resorts, to obtain new ideas of beauty; the poet, to gather inspiration, and the religious teacher to derive from its contemplation, grander conceptions of Deity.

To say, then, as some do, that "Sailors are no better now than they were twenty years ago," that "it is of no use to try any more to save them, heedless and headlong they must go," and that "sailors will be sailors," is as unjust as it is untrue, when applied to those who have been treated as men, and brought under the benificent agencies provided for them by Christian benevolence. And farther still to say, that the youth from our common and Sabbath schools, our academies, and colleges, cannot be formed — under such influences and advantages as a sea life furnish — into a marine, that will do honor to any country on earth, is to deny to education, social culture, morality, and religion, their acknowledged power over human character and destiny; for as has been shown, neither the employments of the sea, its social relations, or its ennobling imagery, tend to debase human character. In conclusion, on this point, the degradation of seamen — whatever the degree, may be safely referred to the adverse influences connected with the unnatural relations into which they are thrown, at the very commencement of their sea life.

THE SAILOR'S TRUE POSITION.

We need, then, as a basis for the improvement of seamen, first of all — that just relations be established between them and their employers, and in raising up a new race of seamen: this result, so much to be desired, may be brought about; and future generations of sailors be made to occupy their true position.

The voluntary system now under consideration, proposes as its first object—*to attach seamen to the employ in which they sail.* This is of first importance, in order to successful effort for improving the character of seamen, and progress in the work of moral elevation, will be marked, by a more intimate acquaintance being formed between the owner and the sailor, than now exists. *This is the great thing to be accomplished.* In other departments of business, as already intimated, the contracting parties know each other, and the relation of employer and employee extends through years, and constitutes the principal element of success. In the counting-room, the work-shop, and factory, parties are brought together, and moral worth as well as skill in the several callings is demanded, and an untiring supervison kept up; and no less an amount of pains-taking will ensure success. But when we come to the contract between the ship and the sailor, these precautionary measures are almost always disregarded, and their object practically defeated, by the employment of an intermediate agency, in no wise identified in interest with the owner; and then comes in the additional evil, that no opportunity is afforded for correcting an error of judgment in the choice of a sailor, when once the ship is at sea.

In attaching seamen to the employ in which they sail, several important advantages will be secured, that will need to be stated separately. The first is, that a higher order of youth will be induced to enter the service. Our first class youth, as a general fact, are detered from going to sea, on account of the prevailing impression that sailors are grossly immoral; these impressions are not entirely without foundation. Take as an illustration the following true picture of the condition of the young sailor, on board many of our vessels at the present day. He finds himself at length upon the deep; the crew are composed, in part, of desperate men, and who, if kept in subjection, require the most despotic government; to which, of necessity, "all hands" must submit. Has he a good "outfit," put up with all a mother's care, and bedewed with a mother's tears! Before the voyage is hardly commenced, he will be robbed of the best portion of it, and who is there, in the present position of parties on board the ship, to redress his wrongs? A statement might be made of cases of this kind, gathered from authentic sources, that would produce indignation in the breast of every right-minded person in community. Now the fact is: that young men with the kind of experience described above,—and such is very common—return home to warn others, but not to go to sea again themselves. One experiment of this sort is quite enough.

Another advantage secured will be — that all *minors*, if they would obtain berths, will be required by the plan, to bring with them certificates from parents or guardians, granting them permission to go to sea. This will operate as a check upon inconsiderate youth, many of whom run away for the purpose of going to sea, a practice no less fatal to their own success, than injurious to the service in which they engage. A youth who, in opposition to the advice, the wishes, and even the authority of a parent, runs away from home, and goes to sea, cannot be expected to make a good sailor; he breaks away from wholesome restraint, violently ruptures every family and kindred tie, alienates fond hearts, and interposes between himself and the home of his childhood, at the very beginning of his career, an insuperable barrier to his return. In an unguarded moment he takes a false step, that cannot be retraced — at least he thinks so — and his language henceforth is, "evil be thou my good." His future course need not be told, nor how a disappointed and chafed spirit becomes a reckless, ungovernable and desperate man. Such is the history of many a noble youth. But instances of this kind will be rare, if encouragement be given to enter the merchant service in a proper and legal manner, and a reasonable assurance afforded parents and guardians, that a youth, on leaving home, to go to sea, will not suffer wrong, but become an object of interest to his employer, as when embarking in other and far less honorable pursuits. The doubt on this point has caused many a parent to withhold consent, and prompted many a youth to run away from home, who otherwise would not; and contributed thereby not a little to the debasement of the native portion of our merchant marine.

A third advantage gained, will be, in the tendency of the plan to diminish the migratory spirit of seamen, which is ever manifesting itself in the desire of change — change of vessel, of voyage, of employment, and which results in an aimless, profitless, wandering life. To correct this unhappy, fatal tendency, the sailor needs the restraints and promptings of domestic life. These he can fully appreciate, and his running away from home — as in some instances — to go to sea, proves nothing to the contrary; the most that can be said, is, that the love of the sea for the time being, is too strong to be controled, and under its influence, as of a rising tide, he is borne away from the family moorings. To diminish, then, the migratory spirit of the sailor, by attaching him to a particular port, which becomes his *home*, and to a particular employ, with which he becomes identified, will be, in effect, to lengthen out his life. And surely something is due to humanity in considering the advantages of the plan proposed. Few sadder sights present, than that of a human being, with ardent affections and sympathies — such as the sailor is known to possess — cut off from the enjoyments of home, and doomed to a wandering life. That the sailor's earthly existence is abridged by reason of this deprivation, no thinking person will, for a moment, doubt. How strong his love of society and of home may be, can only be understood by those who know him best, whose business it has been for years, to entertain him when on shore, and who in the discharge of that duty, have been actuated by a desire to promote his true happiness.

They know, among other things, the sailor's fondness for children, and that he is often as playful as any of them, when relieved from the coercive restraints of a sea life, and full play allowed to the generous impulses of his nature. They know the strength of his attachment to the mistress of the house, that it is almost filial, that he calls her *mother*, that he leaves her often with regret and tears when starting for sea, and on his return hastens to the dwelling where last he laid his weary head, previous to embarking upon an uncertain voyage. The best illustration that can be furnished of the sailor's capacity for domestic life, is found in the superior condition of seamen sailing out of our fishing ports, and the portion of native seamen employed in the coasting trade. And why this superiority? Simply because they have homes on shore, and many of them wives and families. Reference is had here to *common sailors*. It is to the communities where they dwell, and constitute a majority of the population, that we turn with proud exultation, as the evidence of what the mass of sailors may become. And it may well be doubted, whether either the agricultural or manufacturing communities of our State, can furnish a greater number of happy families in proportion to their whole population, or better husbands, fathers or sons, than are found in these communities of sailors.

The last advantage to be named, will be that of correcting the evil connected with advance wages. This is not the place to discuss the question of *Seamen's Advance Wages*, which custom originated among other causes in the necessity of an "*outfit*," and the inability, in numerous instances, from ordinary causes, to provide it — in the destitution accompanying shipwreck, and in the fact that the sailor has no *lien* on the ship for wages in case of the loss of the vessel before freight is earned. "*Freight being the mother of wages.*" The paying advance wages, is not the evil, however, against which so much is said and written, but the abuses growing out of the use made of the money. Let sailors become, then, attached to particular employs; elevate them socially and morally; give them an interest in the vessel, where the thing is possible,* and the instances will be rare of reckless expenditure, and the money, too often squandered in excesses, or alienated by artful villainy, will be deposited in the *Saving's Bank*, or left in trust with the owner.

THE EFFECT UPON THE NAVAL SERVICE.

Another *object aimed at by this plan, is to connect together the mercantile interests and government, in a joint effort to produce an efficient native marine.* The recent Circular of the Secretary of the Treasury, instituting inquiries on several subjects connected with seamen, among others, "*whether it is expedient to require vessels belonging to the United States, and bound on foreign voyages, to take on board apprentices;*" and the recommendations in the Report of the Secretary of the Navy, with regard to the increase of seamen in the Navy, "*to identify them more thoroughly with the Navy, and elevate their character by a plan of rewards as well as punishments,*" the two together, show how absorbing the question of the increase of seamen has become, and how favorable is the present time for practical action on this subject. It is one of the encouraging signs of the times, that government is waking up the importance of doing something to meet the evil. The Report of the Secretary of the Navy, in particular, is a document of great interest, exhibiting alike a high appreciation of the wants of the naval service, and the true value of seamen.

For reasons already stated, there appears to exist insuperable difficulties in the way of an apprenticeship system, either in the merchant or naval service; it is equally plain that the navy must depend mainly upon the merchant marine for its supply of seamen, and consequently that the interests of the two are identical; in these circumstances, it would seem sound policy on the part of government, to encourage and foster the merchant marine. This could be done by a provision of government, (already suggested,)

* See Appendix.

whereby a certificate of faithful service in one employ or more, of from 3 to 5 successive years, with testimonials of good character and seamanship, should entitle the holder to the special consideration and favor of the naval department, and to a preference over all others for employment in the naval service.* This would connect together the merchant and naval service, and give nationality to the entire marine of the country.

THE TIME IS AUSPICIOUS.

Allusion has been made to the attitude of government, as being favorable to present action in the way of improving seamen; elsewhere in different departments of life, the same readiness is discerned. The Savings' Bank for the sailor's hard earnings; the Home for his social nature; the Bethel for his soul; the Sailors' Snug Harbor for his old age; all of which Institutions are established in our midst, invaluable auxiliaries to the carrying forward of rational plans of improvement, and as yet, their power to do good, but partially developed. The increasing regard for the Sabbath among seamen, in this port, will come in to help on the plan proposed. It is a mistake, that sailors want the Sabbath only that they may drink and carouse; the *sailor* is not an infidel, whatever the landsman may be, nor is he less than the beast, who requires the rest designed for him in common with man, and provided for in the commandment, to keep the Sabbath day holy. It is not the case as is sometimes cruelly remarked, "Sailors are too bad to be on shore on the Sabbath, they are better off at sea, where they are out of harm's way; *there,* they cannot disturb the peace of the community." How far this is from being true, is indicated by the fact, that the young men — twenty-five in number — who visit the vessels at the wharves in this city on Sunday mornings, to invite seamen to attend church, meet with a most gratifying reception to their kind invitations. Another kindred fact is, that during six successive summers of preaching on ship-board, I have met but a single instance of serious interruption of the services, and that from well dressed, gentlemanly appearing landsmen.

A NAUTICAL FREE SCHOOL NEEDED.

In addition to the Institutions referred to, one other is needed, to complete the circle, and that is a *Nautical Free School.* The sailor needs cultivation as well as other men, and his efficiency no less than his self-respect requires it; both of which would be promoted by a Free School, where

* See Appendix.

he could spend a month or two of each year of his sea-going life. Many sailors have the desire of improvement, and the means of paying their board, for a few weeks, but cannot meet the additional expense of schooling. In a nautical free school, seamen would acquire a taste for reading and study, which would go to sea with them, and prove of incalculable advantage to all concerned. A library might be added, from which books, in limited numbers, could be obtained, taken to sea, and returned at the close of the voyage — the common branches of education might be taught there, with navigation, and other studies of most practical benefit. My experience among seamen for upwards of thirty years, has satisfied me of the existence of this great want. How such an Institution may be provided, is not difficult to determine. An endowment of $100,000, would do it all, (the amount invested in some of our clipper ships,) and probably it would *pay* as well as the best of them. Why should not the government foster such Institutions in all our large seaports, by appropriations from the public Treasury? not with the view to exercise control over them, for in the ever-changing phases of parties, and of policy, under a free government, a benevolent reformatory institution would either suffer from neglect, or be wrecked by bad management. Nothing can be plainer, than that such an Institution can only prosper when under the supervision and influence of those who enter into the spirit of the design, and espouse the interest as their own. Might not the suggestions of the late Secretary of the Navy, in relation to the Naval Academy, and the inquiry of the present Secretary of the Treasury, based on a resolution of the Senate of the United States at its last session, — "*Whether it is expedient to establish, by law, Schools of Instruction for mariners, or such as are preparing to enter into that service,*" find practical illustration in such a plan; might not the initiatory preparation for the naval academy be effected in this way, and the best material for the posts of honor in our navy be found in these schools? The improvement in the sailor's condition on ship-board, in substituting light and airy rooms on deck, in place of the dark, damp, and often noisome forecastle, is promotive of his comfort, and self-respect, induces contentment, and helps on a reform.

The increasing travel by sea, is not without its improving influence. The monotony of the sea is broken in upon by intelligent intercourse, and a pleasing variety imparted to sea life, and when passengers are intelligent and judicious — by means of books, instruction, and conversation, much may be done for the sailor's good, during the voyage.

The demand for a higher order of men to sail our princely clipper ships, comes in to help on the work of improvement. Great stress is laid on heroism in the saving of life at sea, and well it may be, for life is of more value than all else ; and he who risks life to save life, other things being equal, is the man to command a ship. The recent disasters at sea, and the heroism displayed, have served to bring out character, and to show us what kind of men is needed. The responsibilities of officers of late years, have greatly increased ; the evidence of the fact is found in the increased pay. Mates of ships now receive $50 and 60 per month, who, twenty years ago, received only $30. Hence a higher order of seamen is demanded, as a foundation for a high order of officers ; this is seen and felt.

The position of Boston among other things, is favorable for commencing *here* the work of improvement. Equal to any other seaport of the United States, in the quality of her shipping, she is in advance of all others, in respect to the employment of means for elevating the character of her marine, which will compare favorably with that of any other port in the world. Why should she not, then, occupy the front rank in a reform so humane, so in keeping with her past history and present position, and so intimately connected with her highest interests ? It is in the power of Boston ship-owners, should they undertake this work *alone*, to drive every unprincipled or worthless sailor to some other port, to find employment, and draw to themselves the best men that float upon the deep.

THE MATERIAL IS ABUNDANT.

We are eminently a maritime people ; the love of the sea, as already remarked, is a passion with many of our youth. Applications for voyages are being constantly made at this office and elsewhere in the city, by the finest young men and boys, from all parts of the State, and I doubt not that among them, are many who, had they but the opportunity, would develop a character as noble as that of the lamented Captain Richardson, of the Staffordshire. The run upon the "Great Republic," at New York,* is a fine illustration of the feeling existing ; hundreds of young men and boys of the highest respectability, from all parts of the State, offering their services as voluntary apprentices or green hands.

* See Appendix.

A question arises here, of some importance to the proper understanding of this subject. *To what extent is it either safe or profitable to employ green hands and ordinary seamen, on board our merchant ships?* This question can best be answered by employers and ship-masters, as their own judgment and interest may dictate. It is known that in the whale fisheries, the proportion of green hands to able seamen, is often very large; and although such proportion would not answer for the West India or European trade, there is less to object to it, in voyages across the Equator, where time and good weather combine, to help forward the green hand in learning ship's duty. There is a question, too, regarding the relative value of able and ordinary seamen. On this point, experienced ship-masters, who have commanded both large and small vessels, express the opinion, *that ambitious young men, actually become as good sailors in one year, as the average of the crews usually shipped for able seamen at full wages.* The Captain of a first class clipper ship, states, that in a late voyage to the Pacific, the only portion of his crew, on whom he could rely, were the boys who had sailed with him in a previous voyage; the rest of the crew deserting the ship as soon as she arrived at her outward port. Other ship-masters have had similar experiences. One ship-master referred to a young man who shipped with him as a green hand, and who performed two voyages to the Pacific, during which time, unaided by friends, he qualified himself for a second mate's berth on board a first class clipper ship, for which he recommended him. It is probably within the recollection of many, that a few years since, a lad on board an American East Indiaman, was thrust into the command of the ship on the homeward voyage, by reason of the death of the officers; this lad, by his skillful management, and knowledge of navigation, brought the vessel safely into port.

As to the difficulty attending the creation of able seamen out of green hands, it need not be greater than that of raising up good carpenters and masons from the raw material; but was it even four-fold greater, it would need to be done, *or a substitute found for sailors.* The training of young men for able seamen, is doubtless one of the most important duties that an officer of a vessel can be called upon to discharge, and one as highly promotive of the interests of the owner. "Young men for soldiers," said Napoleon, and tyrant though he was, he made the young men love as well as obey him. Here the motto is, "young men for sailors," and the power of the ship-master, in his particular sphere, to mould at will the young men under his command, is not less than that of the great warrior. Indeed, a nobler duty is rarely presented, than that of training up high spirited, intelligent youth, to bear the flag of our country, with honor, to the ends of the earth.

THE NECESSITY IS URGENT.

How urgent the necessity of a plan for the employment of *green hands*, has become, will be seen in the fact, that *the system now in full operation, employs a greater number than is contemplated in the plan proposed;* but the material is so insufferably bad, as to endanger navigation. And this is in no wise strange ; men are wanted of some sort, and must be had, and as green hands are rejected, as such, they must, of necessity, be shipped as *able seamen.* A common experience of ship-masters' of late, has been, that full one-half of their crews, on getting to sea, are found incapable of taking the helm. The question then is not, whether we will have green hands on board our vessels, that is settled ; but what shall be the character of those we employ. Recent occurrences show the extremity which has been reached. A New York Packet Ship, on her way to London, recently, put into this port to replenish her crew, twelve of whom were unable to go aloft. A ship-master in writing to the Sailor's Magazine, a few months since, furnishes a description of the crews that sailed with him in two successive voyages to the Pacific ; the whole number composing these two crews, was forty-five, of which twenty-one were ignorant of ship's duty, and most of them entirely useless. All but one of these twenty-one persons, were shipped as *able seamen,* at full wages. The amount of advance wages charged to the ship, on their account, was $415 ; out of which they were allowed, by those who shipped them, $41 in clothing—*two dollars each*—but not a dollar in money ; their moral character, and the condition of their wardrobe, sorted well with each other ; they were both execrably bad ; one died with delirium tremens, before getting out of the bay, and another fell off the jib-boom in the East River, probably from the same cause, and was drowned. Humanity shudders at such a frightful picture, and asks, how long shall these things be ? And yet this is but the natural working of the present system, and its legitimate results.* The question finally is, which is preferable, men of the description above, at full wages, or young men of good character, intelligence and ambition, at half the price ?

* See Appendix.

WILL THE PLAN DIMINISH THE EXPENSES AND RISKS OF NAVIGATION?

This last point is of equal interest with either of the preceding. The question has respect to the wages of seamen, which constitute an important item in the expenses of the ship, and is therefore one of grave importance.

It is sometimes argued that the lowest rate of seamen's wages is best, as affording less temptation to extravagance. In reference to the reckless sailor, this may, to some extent, be true, alas! the fact. But the results of Seamens' Savings Banks, and other aids to social improvement and thrift in late years, have removed this reproach from seamen, as a class. In considering the sailors' claim of wages, his services should be compared with those of other men in other employments, requiring equal skill and labor. It will be conceded by all who are informed on the subject, that the good *marline-spike* sailor will compare favorably with the ship carpenter, the caulker and graver, the rope and sail maker, the rigger, the stevedore, the painter, in several of which arts he is found often to be well skilled. In some circumstances, his services are incomparably more valuable than either of the mechanics named; a good *helmsman*, in a gale of wind on board a richly freighted vessel, with many passengers, not only commands our admiration, but richly deserves the highest wages paid a Railroad engineer.

The labors of those several classes of mechanics, are of no more pressing necessity, than those of seamen; require no more skill, and infinitely less toil, self-denial and exposure. Neither have they a single demand for money, that every seaman does not share in common with them. Some of each of these classes are married and have families, but this furnishes no exception to the sailors' claim of wages; the design of marriage was to bless mankind, sailors as well as landsmen, and the neglect or deprivation of this beneficent institution, with all its solemn responsibilities and refining and purifying influences, has been the procuring cause of much of the sailor's moral degradation. The Captain of a ship who returns to his family at the close of the voyage, the mate to his, the steward to his—no more need, and have no better claim to the blessings of a home and a family than the seamen belonging to the same ship; both the one and the other have a social and moral nature that need to be cultivated; civil rights to exercise; a name and place among the living, to be sacredly preserved. An ancient philosopher, in distributing the human race into two classes, the living and the dead, inquires, "Who can determine in which class we are to enter the name of those on the sea?"

If the sailor, however, chooses to remain unmarried, then he needs all his surplus wages to lengthen the period of his stay on shore; ten months out of every twelve, spent amid the solitudes of the ocean, is too large a proportion of the sailor's brief and stormy life. He needs the Sabbath on shore, with all its rich privileges; time to make acquaintance and form friendships; to see the sights of the town; read the journals of the day, and learn his true position and importance among men. He needs leisure for general reading, and intellectual improvement, and recreation among the green fields and singing birds of the country. Especially does he need to visit the home of his childhood, to look upon the face of his mother, be enfolded again in her loving embrace, and allowed to prove to all, that he is not recreant to his earliest and best instincts; and that he has virtue, manhood and love of home still ruling his true heart. All this, and more, that requires money, the sailor needs, as the means for promoting his happiness, increasing his efficiency, and lengthening out his days, which are fewer by far than those of other men. And should there remain at any time "a shot in the locker," he will have learnt how to secure it against a rainy day. Superadded to the foregoing is the melancholy fact, that the sailor, unlike either of the classes of mechanics alluded to, is subject to *total loss* by shipwreck.

If the view here taken be just, and seamen both earn and require, including their board, the wages paid other men for services demanding equal labor and skill; then it is just that they should receive them, and no plan for increasing the number of seamen, or improving their character, can be expected fully to succeed, if this principle be overlooked. As regards the rate of seamen's wages, we have nothing to do, the object being solely to estimate and compare their services with those of other mechanics. But to the question — *Will the plan diminish the expenses and risks of Navigation?* Of this, there can scarcely be a doubt. The result will be brought about by elevating and ennobling the employment, and raising it to the commanding position which it is destined to occupy among the honorable pursuits of the day; and thus obviating the objections to a sea life entertained by a large portion of community, and securing the services of the choicest youth of our land. By combining green hands and ordinary seamen in the composition of a crew, and thereby decreasing the average rate of wages; by diminishing the number of desertions abroad, and the expenses consequent thereon; by securing cheerful and prompt obedience to orders, inducing happiness "fore and aft," putting an end to insubordination and violence, and expensive and vexatious lawsuits; by diminishing the migratory spirit of seamen, and attaching them to one port and one employ; and by the increased care, vigilance, and devotion of a crew, indentified in interest with the owner.*

CIRCULAR.

Frequent applications are made at this Office, by young men and boys, residing out of the city, for information and aid, in obtaining sea voyages.

With the view of meeting these demands in a way to benefit the applicants, and at the same time promote the benevolent objects of this mission, an agency has been established at this Office, whereby much of the delay and expense of a visit to the city, occasioned by the want of information may be avoided.

Applications by letter may be made to the Office, to contain the residence, age, physical peculiarities, and past and present employments — if any — of the parties. All of which will be registered in a book kept for that purpose; the letters in every instance to be marked "Ship," on the envelope, and the postage paid. Sickly, or feeble persons, or boys under sixteen years of age, need not apply.

Applicants will be informed by mail or otherwise, of vessels wanting hands; the nature of the voyage; probable wages, and time of sailing; and they will hold themselves in readiness to leave their homes *promptly*. Those who visit the city, with the intention of going to sea, will do so at their own expense and risk; they will bring with them testimonials of good character from responsible persons; and if *minors*, will require in addition a certificate from parents or guardians, properly attested, consenting to their going to sea. Applications made at the Office, *in person*, will be promptly attended to, and counsel and advice given in relation to boarding house and outfit.

THOMAS V. SULLIVAN, Missionary.

OFFICE OF THE MARINE MISSION AT LARGE,
No. 8 LONG WHARF.

Boston, January 1, 1854.

* See Appendix.

The following communication will serve to show in what estimation the plan is held by practical seamen.

New York, Dec. 24, 1853.

CAPT. THOMAS V. SULLIVAN, Marine Missionary, Boston:

Dear Sir:—Your plan received to-day, for increasing the number and efficiency of American seamen, strikes me favorably, and I most heartily wish you success in your laudable undertaking. Command my services in any way in which I can serve you.

The boys you furnished me for the Great Republic, are doing well.

(Signed,) L. McKAY.

In submitting the foregoing views, and the line of duty indicated, your Missionary would guard against any misconception that might arise, in respect to the position to be assumed by this Mission, before the public. To make this clear, he would state, that it is not proposed to open a SHIPPING OFFICE, to compete with those now existing: for this, there is no time to spare from the work of the Mission. The objects aimed at are set forth in the Circular. In pursuing them, certain results will be expected to follow. Among others, that youth, desiring to go to sea, may do so without having to spend their money in unavailing efforts to find employment, or making the doubtful experiment of running away from home; in either case subjecting themselves to disappointment and all its vicious and debasing tendencies, and to the liability of falling victims to designing men. By this means, the fear of parents will be allayed, objections to their son's going to sea removed, and ship owners and ship-masters who desire it (and their numbers are fast increasing,) may obtain green hands of reliable character.

With reference to undertaking this work, your Missionary would gladly have looked on, and rejoiced in the efforts of others; but no one entered the field. To state the want merely, as in the foregoing pages, was theory alone, a practical effort in connection therewith was demanded. The position of the Mission is favorable to the undertaking, the direct result will be an enlarged acquaintance with those, whose welfare you are seeking to promote. As regards the measure of success, time will determine that; a beginning has already been made. The want is great; to do any thing, however small, to meet that want—***is success.***

The whole subject is submitted to the consideration of your Committee, and to the friends of Seamen generally. The additional work marked out, will greatly increase the usefulness of the Mission, and add something to its expenses which it is hoped and believed will be promptly met by an appreciating public.

REPORT OF LABORS AND RESULTS.

The operations of the Mission since the last published Report, have been of the same general character, as in previous years, and attended with encouraging results. The attendance at the religious ship-board services on the Sabbath, at 9 A. M. and 5 P. M., has been good, and the visitation of vessels at the wharves, early Sabbath mornings, has been carried forward with constantly increasing efficiency. Twenty-five young men, all members of churches in the city, and all volunteers, have been zealously engaged in the work in sunshine and in storm, distributing religious tracts, and in extending to seamen the kindly invitation to attend church, and the blessings of many ready to perish have come upon them.

The labors on ship-board have been prosecuted with vigor. Many valuable acquaintances have been made with officers and seamen, and influences set at work calculated to do good socially and morally. Among the agencies employed in this department is that of supplying vessels gratuitously with books and other reading matter for the use of the crews at sea, especially those bound on long voyages. The following extract of a letter from the Captain of a first class clipper, exhibits the nature of the work.

East Boston, Nov. 12, 1853.

Capt. Thos. V. Sullivan,—Dear Sir: I have received your very handsome present of most useful books. I have examined them and think that they are much better selected than any other lot ever put on board any vessel which I have commanded. You will pardon me for saying that I think the selection of books usually made for sailors are not wisely selected; they consist almost entirely of Bibles, Testaments, Prayer Books, and Tracts, all of which are invaluable treasures. But sailors are like other folks, at least not more religious, and they want useful reading matter that will enlist them. Yours, truly.

These books, beside an assortment of Bibles in thirteen different languages spoken among seamen, contained four volumes of Tracts prepared by this Mission, each volume containing ten different languages, an assortment of moral and religious, entertaining and instructing books, with a set of School Books to meet the wants of all on board, who might desire to improve themselves from the A, B, C, of knowledge up to the study of Latin and Greek. A most gratifying result in connection with these efforts has been the hearty coöperation of ship-masters.

THE ISSUES FROM THE OFFICE OF THE MISSION,

For the past five years, including the supplying of seamen calling at the Office, have been 3138 Bibles and Testaments, 21,983 volumes of Books, and 86,103 copies of moral and religious periodical literature, and over one and a half million pages of religious and temperance Tracts.

MARINE FREE CIRCULATING LIBRARY.

Allusion has been made to the want of a "Nautical Free School" in this city, and in connection therewith a Library, "from which books in limited numbers might be obtained, taken to sea and returned at the close of the voyage." As regards the School, it may prove the work of time, although its importance must be manifest. In any case its final establishment may be considered as certain as that of either the Mariner's Church, the Savings' Bank, — the Sailors' Home, or the Sailors Snug Harbor. But there need be no delay in respect to the Library; the experience of past years in gathering and distributing books gratuitously, among seamen, shows conclusively that there are books enough to be had; and the fact, that four thousand books could be collected and distributed annually among seamen for five successive years, without any increase of difficulty in obtaining them; is worthy of being recorded. It is a fact too of special encouragement when viewed in connection with an attempt to establish a Marine Free Circulating Library.

Guided then by past experience, and trusting in him "who turneth the heart as the rivers of water, and as the streams in the South," your Missionary will go forward in the endeavor to establish a Marine Free Circulating Library in connection with this Mission, and henceforth it will receive a share of his thoughts and efforts.

The principle of a Free Circulating Library has been in operation in connection with this Mission for several years. Many books have been loaned to seamen calling at the office, and read and returned. And with the view of carrying out the principle as now proposed; books from time to time have been selected from the thousands of volumes sent to this office for gratuitous distribution, and set apart as the nucleus of a Library. In future receipts of books at the office, other selections will be made from time to time, and from this source, and from donations made expressly to the Library, it is confidently expected, that in good time, the object aimed at will be accomplished; and that no sailor will have occasion to go to sea, from Boston, without a few interesting and instructive books to read during the voyage.

It is not expected that the books of such a library will in the circumstances, *last* so long, or the Library itself retain through successive years its catalogue of books entire, as in the case of Libraries generally. The most that can be done or desired will be, to require a trifling deposit of those taking out books, to induce their return; and when worn out with the rough usage of the sea, or neglected to be returned; then, to call upon a benevolent public for new supplies. The friends of seamen have yet to learn, that there is a point, in the prosecution of wise and beneficent plans for promoting the sailor's welfare, where the public sentiment existing among us, will not fully justify and sustain the effort.

In entering upon the work of establishing a Marine Free Circulating Library, the idea is, to anticipate a forthcoming Nautical Free School, and that the Library ultimately be donated to that Institution. Donations of books are respectfully solicited for the Library, from city and country, which may be sent to the Office. Friends of seamen in the city having books to bestow, by addressing a line to the Missionary, through the Post Office, will be waited upon, and their books removed without causing them trouble. New books and those which have been read and handled, if in good condition, will be gratefully received, and duly acknowledged. Donors of books will please insert their names upon each volume, that seamen may know who are their friends.

BENEVOLENCE.

The weekly visits at the Marine Hospital have been continued. These labors are purely religious and benevolent, and consist in holding religious conversation, distributing the Scriptures and other religious reading, corresponding with the friends of those, who from any cause are unable to write, inciting the ignorant to learn to read, and supplying them with books, furnishing clothing to the destitute, and assisting the incurable and decrepit to obtain entrance to the Sailors' Snug Harbor. Occasional visits have been made to the House of Industry, and to Deer Island, to succor some unfortunate sailor who has "brought up" in either of those institutions, and numerous calls of the shipwrecked and suffering have been attended to at the Office.

The resources of the Mission for usefulness, are on the increase. From the friends of seamen in city and country, clothing for the destitute, and books for gratuitous distribution are being received. There is as yet no perceptible limit in the extent to which labor in these directions may be carried. It is hoped that the friends of the Mission will furnish the means of enlarged effort.

Since the last Report, two of the earliest friends of the Mission have been called from time to eternity. One of these, Capt. Josiah Bacon, was an original member of your Committee, which relation he sustained at the time of his death. By means of his official position as Steward of Chelsea Marine Hospital—his warm hearted benevolence, his deep interest in the sailor's welfare, and his mature and comprehensive judgment, he greatly aided the operations of this Mission, and when at length he was no longer permitted in his relations here and in others kindred, to do the sailor good, he evinced the sincerity of his devotion, by making seamen the heirs to his worldly estate. "The Sailor's Snug Harbor of Boston," is an enduring memorial of his single-hearted, unostentatious benevolence.

The other friend alluded to, was the late Capt. Josiah Richardson, of the ship Staffordshire. His cheerful smile, his open handed, open hearted benevolence, are among the cherished recollections — the green spots, of years of toilsome effort in the seamens' cause. His friendship is enbalmed in the heart a sacred deposit — his words of encouragement and hopefulness still linger in the memory, a vitalizing principle of future action.

In closing this Report, your Missionary would acknowledge, with gratitude, the favor of God, which has attended this enterprise in every stage of its progress. Commencing nearly six years ago, at first an experiment, the work has continued on to the present time. The effort can no longer be considered in the light of an experiment. To preach the Gospel to seamen on shipboard, on the Sabbath; to visit them through the agency of Christian young men on board their floating homes on Sabbath morning, inviting them to the house of God, scattering the religious Tract, and directing the unfortunate and destitute to where they may find friends — to get the confidence of the humble but trusting Christian sailor, place before him motives to effort for the salvation of the soul of his shipmate, and furnish him with the means of doing good — to send the Bible, the Tract, History, Biography, and other good and instructive reading on a tour of benevolence around the world — to seek out and relieve human suffering in the Marine Hospital, the Poor House and elsewhere, and obtain for the worn out and decrepit sailor a home in the Sailors' Snug Harbor; such cannot be a work of experiment merely, but one of permanent interest and importance.

All of which is respectfully submitted.

THOMAS V. SULLIVAN.

TREASURER'S REPORT.

Marine Mission at Large in Account with J. S. BARBOUR, Treas'r.

To amount paid Capt. T. V. Sullivan, on account of Salary for two years' Services, ...	$1734 79		
" amount due on account of of Salary, ...	265 21		
" " paid for Office Expenses, Rent, Assistant, Expenses for Books, and in Benevolent Department, ...	538 06		
" " due January 1, 1852, ...	820 46		
		$3358 52	

Contra Cr.

By amount collected from various sources, ...	2272 85	
" balance due, ...	1085 67	
		$3358 52

J. S. BARBOUR, Treasurer.

FREDERICK D. ALLEN, Auditor.

Boston, January 1, 1854.

The Report of our Missionary for the last two years, is herewith submitted to the public. The body of the Report is occupied in discussing the subject of the present "Scarcity of Seamen," which it is admitted is one of commanding interest, and the hope is entertained that it will prove timely and beneficial. The Treasurer's Report is subjoined, showing a deficit of $1085.67, notwithstanding the rigid economy observed in conducting the affairs of the Mission — the results of which, have been truly gratifying, and strongly contrast with the sum expended in securing them. The present debt of the Mission is the aggregated deficiences of successive years, and has originated, in a reluctance to employ a paid agency to collect funds, dependence being placed mainly on voluntary contributions.

The sum required to meet the expenses of the current year and pay off the debt, is $2500.00. There will be occasion to employ extra agencies, including the press, in carrying out the plans suggested in the Report, creating thereby extra demands for funds which we look to a benevolent public to supply. To all interested in Navigation, the Committee would respectfully commend this benevolent work. For six years the Mission has been quietly and unostentatiously pursuing its labor of love among the shipping in the Port of Boston, and one of the results has been the gratuitous circulation of over 20,000 volumes of Books and other valuable reading matter. Is it too much to ask, in view of such a fact, that you would extend to the Mission a helping hand, in its present time of need?

The friends of seamen in the country, into whose hands this Report may fall, are reminded that this Mission contemplates among its benevolent designs to promote the welfare of their sons and brothers who visit the city with the intention of going to sea, will you not help us? To Clergymen, in a particular manner, would we commend this benevolent work, and solicit their valuable co-operation in obtaining pecuniary aid. To all who feel interested in the Sailor's welfare for time and eternity, we commend the work of the Mission, in confidence and in hope.

Donations sent to the Treasurer, James S. Barbour, No. 30 Court Street, or either of the Committee, will be gratefully received and duly acknowledged.

COMMITTEE.

JOTHAM STETSON, WILLIAM BLAKE,
JOHN GOVE, EDWARD S. TOBEY,
CLEMENT DREW, FREDERICK D ALLEN,
AARON BREED, PLINY NICKERSON,
PEARL MARTIN, GEORGE HOWLAND.

JAMES S. BARBOUR, Treasurer.

WM. W. MAIR, Secretary.

☞ An unavoidable delay in getting out this Report, has furnished opportunity for obtaining facts of recent occurrence, which will be found in the Appendix.

APPENDIX.

ILLUSTRATIVE FACTS.

MATERIAL ENOUGH FOR GREEN HANDS.

New York, December 26th, 1853.

Capt. Thos. V. Sullivan, Boston:—Dear Sir,—I have received your kind note * * * * I have a goodly number of boys, about forty. The Journal of Commerce of this city has a paragraph, stating the fact that the ship was to take out a good number of young men. I think that I have had hundreds of applications, nearly all through this notice. I get a batch of letters every day from all parts of the country, all referring to this notice; proving most conclusively that there is material enough in this country, if it was only brought into shape, to make sailors for all our ships. I am, in haste, your Friend,

L. McKAY.

The want of Able Seamen is general.—Among the numerous disasters by sea during the present winter, attended with a sad loss of human life, the recent wreck of the English ship Tayleur, on the Coast of Ireland, stands conspicuous. The Tayleur was a new ship, constructed of Iron, of more than 2000 tons, and sailed from Liverpool for Australia, with a valuable cargo, and a large number of passengers. She experienced a heavy gale in the Channel, and went on shore at Lambay, in the vicinity of Dublin Bay. The whole number of souls on board, are stated to have been 660, of which 282 only were saved. Of those lost 250 were women and children. The loss of the vessel was generally attributed to errors in the compass, and to the inefficiency of her crew, fifteen only out of fifty men were able seamen. The crew included Chinese and Lascars, who were unable to understand the English language, and the orders were therefore imperfectly executed. The vessel is said to have drifted about at the mercy of the winds and waves, for several hours before the wreck.

The idea not unfrequently entertained and expressed is, that "seamen cannot be influenced by proper motives to do right." This is a libel on the whole class, and bears alike on officers and seamen. There is a strange inconsistency here. It is common to speak of sailors—"as a class of noble, generous hearted men, who will go any lengths to serve a friend, or deny themselves to benefit others; as the soul of honor, chivalrous and gallant, and in their way polite," and yet, these same men, from among whom a larger proportion of nature's noblemen may be produced than from any other equal portion of the human race, "cannot be influenced by motives to do right"—cannot be treated with as other men, have no appreciation of kindness, and as little of the value of property; that they are too migratory in spirit to become attached to any particular place; and more of the same sort which might be named. But time, and a better knowledge of the sailor, than is now generally possessed, will set this matter right, and we can well afford to wait the event. For the present, by way of commentary on the general subject, and with the design more fully to illustrate certain points brought to view in the foregoing pages, a few illustrative facts are furnished which may assist in giving completeness to the view taken.

The Sailor needs an interest in the Ship.—Why should he not have it, if it will be for his benefit, and that of the owners? The principle of fractional joint interest in the ship, or in her earnings, by the common sailor, is no new doctrine, it prevails to some extent among the Eastern vessels, and is general in the Cod, the Mackerel, and Whale Fisheries; in the latter, not always to the advantage of the sailor. We hear of small "Lays," long voyages with much wear and tear, and an inflated "slop chest," and sometimes the sailor, at the end of a three year's voyage, finds himself "astern the lighter." Nevertheless, the principle in itself is good—good for the sailor as for the principal owner; were it not, Commerce and the Fisheries would be at an end. It is only when the arrangement between the parties is inequitable, and bears unjustly on the sailor, that the principle works badly. Applied to the case of the sailor in the merchant ship, it works as follows:

A retired ship-master relates of himself, that "during the period in which he sailed 'before the mast,' he made a voyage in a Salem East Indiaman, to Sumatra, and thence to Europe. On board that ship the custom prevailed, of allowing to each of the crew a half ton privilege, to be filled with the Sailor's Venture; the Captain effecting sales on the sailors' account without charge. Navigation also, was taught on board by the officers. As the result of all this pains-taking to benefit seamen, nearly all of that crew subsequently became officers of vessels."

The recognition of this principle, and the progressive tendencies of the age, will be seen in the following extracts from a plan brought forward in Philadelphia, in January of the present year, where joint ownership by seamen associated together, is proposed to be carried out, on a scale never before attempted. Of the probable success of the plan on so large a scale, it may be premature to speak.

"PROSPECTUS OF THE

SEAMENS' NAVIGATION COMPANY OF AMERICA.

This Company has been established for the further advancement and elevation of the mariners of the merchant service of the United States, and upon such a basis as will enable seamen, by an association and union of labor and capital, to become joint owners and navigators of vessels in which they may be employed. The capital is fixed at $500,000, divided into 10,000 shares, at $50 each.

It shall have for its object, the accumulation of a sufficient fund, by means of periodical instalments from its members, to purchase sailing or steam vessels, to be manned and officered by members of the Company. The profits and earnings arising from said vessels, to be divided among the stockholders at such times and in such manner as hereinafter specified."

The Sailor needs to know his Employer.—This is the privilege of the mechanic on shore, and why should it not be of the sailor at sea? The former needs not the countenance and favor of his employer as does the sailor. Around him is thrown every needed safeguard, his every interest, personal and social, his own proper manhood included are protected by law; and the conventionalities of society. How different the condition of the sailor — a homeless wanderer, every where a stranger, his character and claims seldom understood, or at least not acknowledged. To him, kindness is as rare as flowers in mid winter, and as grateful when met with. A ship-master, who commenced his sea life about the time of the discovery of South Shetland, and who made his first voyage to that inhospitable region, relates the following incident to illustrate the effect of kindness and attention on the part of a ship-owner. "The gentleman (who understood sailors better than some who rail against them,) accompanied the ship down the harbor and returned with the pilot. While on board he addressed the crew on the nature of the voyage, spoke of his own expectations and hopes, and expressed his confidence in the ability and good conduct of the crew as the main dependence in the making of a voyage. The effect of that well timed, benevolent speech, was like magic, and of a large ship's company of men and boys, there was not one that did not feel its full force, or that was not influenced by it for good, during the long and most unpleasant voyage."

Sailors can be trusted.—In the sweeping charges often brought against sailors, the exceptions made are usually rare, and few in number those who are admitted to possess redeeming traits of character. This is most unfortunate, as it operates to the injury of the whole class, and tends to depress, rather than to stimulate and encourage to an honorable course. A ship-master furnishes the following, to illustrate the readiness of seamen generally to do right, when properly influenced. For several years "he run a packet between New York and a port in South America. The custom then, as now, was to load and unload with stevedores, the crew being discharged immediately on the return of the vessel to her port, where there was a detention ordinarily of from three to four weeks. Becoming at length wearied with bad crews, he ventured on an experiment and shipped a crew of average moral character, selected from a number of men sent on board by the shipping officer, and went to sea. On setting the watches at night, the men were called together, and he addressed them briefly, in regard to their duty, and promised them, on his part, kind and just treatment. They had never before been treated thus, and it surprised and won them. On entering port, at the close of the voyage, they came aft in a body and asked permission to stay by the vessel, discharge her cargo, load, and go to sea in her again.

The proposition was submitted to the owner, but he objected, he had no faith, he said, in sailors. The captain urged the suit of his crew, to whom he had become attached, and the owner at length consented. They staid by the ship, and more than realized the expectations entertained of them. They made repeated voyages in the same vessel under his command, doing their duty like men when at sea, and when in port proving the best of ship-keepers and stevedores, with much saving of expense to the ship, and of anxiety and trouble to owners and officers."

GOOD OFFICERS MAKE GOOD MEN.

The Noble Commodore.—The following account of an interesting occurrence which took place in this city in November, 1845, and which created no little sensation at the time, is taken from the "Boston Post." It speaks for itself.

"The crew of the United States Frigate Cumberland at this port, preceded by the brass band, and bearing aloft at regular intervals the National flag, walked in procession to the United States Hotel, to pay their parting respects to their beloved Commodore. The sailors were dressed in blue jackets and trowsers, white frocks with blue collars, and black hats with the frigate's name on the bands. The farewell salutation of the tars, and the reply of the gallant Commodore, to use one of father Taylor's phrases—'were all soul,' and the cheers and music blending, sent up parting echoes that were heard miles distant. Nothing can be more morally true than the old saying, that good officers make good men"—and visa versa.

The following Act it is proposed to submit to the Congress of the United States, now in session:

Be it enacted by the Senate and House of Representatives of the United States, in Congress assembled, and by the authority of the same—

Section 1. That every native born or naturalized citizen of the United States, who shall serve from three to five years next preceding legal manhood, in the merchant marine of the United States, and obtain written testimonials from his employers, properly attested, of faithful service, good character and seamanship, shall be entitled to the consideration of government, *as an able seaman,* and to such privileges and preference in connection with the Naval and Revenue Service as the fostering patronage of Government, from time to time may direct, or the exigencies of the Naval or Revenue Service may require.

Section 2. A certificate of able seamanship as provided in the foregoing Act, shall be furnished by the Collector of Customs of the District sailed from, to every applicant authorized to receive it; and a *Registry of Able Seamen* shall be kept in each District, for the information and use of the Government.

Press of J. Howe, 39 Merchants Row, Boston.

www.ingramcontent.com/pod-product-compliance
Lightning Source LLC
LaVergne TN
LVHW011126110826
845150LV00008B/2261

* 9 7 8 1 4 1 8 1 9 5 0 7 6 *